TOTALLY WEIRD ACTIVITY Bo

Creative Coloring and Far-out Fun!

Created by illustrator Mark Penta & writer T.M. Murphy

WEST MARGIN PRESS

ISBN: 9781513134901

Printed in China
1 2 3 4 5 6 7 8 9 10

Published by West Margin Press®

WEST
MARGIN
PRESS
WestMarginPress.com

Proudly distributed by Ingram Publisher Services

WEST MARGIN PRESS
Publishing Director: Jennifer Newens
Marketing Manager: Alice Wertheimer
Project Specialist: Micaela Clark
Editor: Olivia Ngai
Design & Production: Rachel Lopez Metzger

Coloring Tips!

We hope you have fun coloring the pages in this book!

The back of every coloring page is blank for two reasons:

1. So your colors won't leak through to the next drawing.

2. So you can use the empty page to finish writing your stories.

Want your pages to look really cool?

• Use colored pencils or crayons.

• Find coloring packages with different skin colors.

• If you use markers or paints, be sure to put a thick piece of paper underneath the pages you color.

THE STAN CAM... ADVENTURE!

STAN the cat was always running off somewhere. His family attached a video camera to his collar so they could watch his adventures unfold!

In the spaces below, draw the things Stan saw during his six-day disappearance!

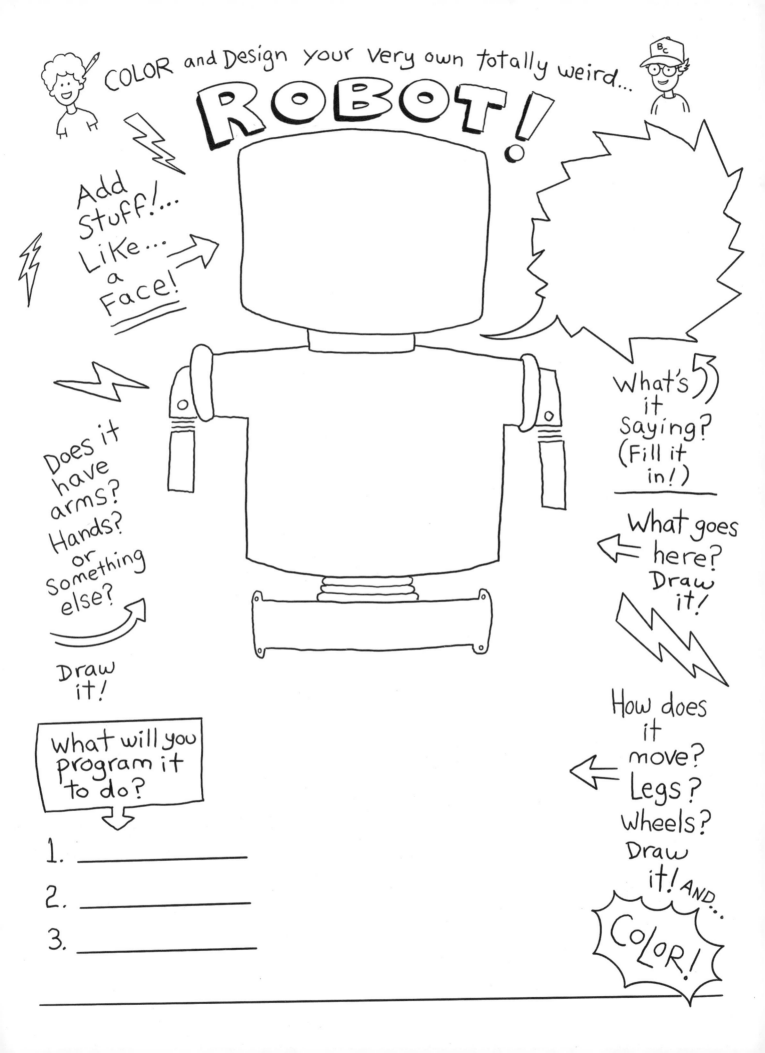

Hey! It's the TOTALLY WEIRD (and warped!) WORD SEARCH!

Find and circle **10** words with the theme: "THINGS CREATIVE PEOPLE DO!"

Far out!

```
I N V E N T D O B D
A Y T U W Y R T D L
B D R U W Y R T D L
F E O A W C E D A P
H X E P R E D A P
P A M R B A U N M
G S I I L M V C I M
R C C N T J F Y C I M
Q V Y E K F Y E Z A
U F G M K G X Z A
A L R M N A T R G
M P X K I J S O R G
Z T K S V L S R I
  Z C W A O W L S M N
    C W O G J A E
        Q L Z V
```

SPELLA the Witch is making some alphabet soup. Help her UNJUMBLE the letters so she can serve up some frightening fun to her friends!

And color the page!

Hint!: These are SPOOKY-themed words!

① TBSA ② HTOGS ③ BZMIOE

④ LEESTOKN ⑤ VARGEDYAR

⑥ RWWOFLEE

UNSCRAMBLE THE LETTERS HERE!

① _____ ② _____ ③ _____

④ _____ ⑤ _____ ⑥ _____

Write a story inside Miss Madari's scary house using **3** words from the jumble on the previous page!

‹(STORY TITLE)›

NO TRESPASSING

It all started one morning when...

* Turn the page to finish!

CREATE a TOTALLY WEIRD SUPERHERO!

DESIGN and COLOR their COSTUME!

What's their Symbol?

How did they become a Superhero?

_____
_____
_____

Who do they protect?

_____
_____

What are their powers?

_____
_____
_____

What's their Weakness?

_____
_____
_____

Where are they from?

_____

Where is their hideout?

_____
_____

_____
SUPERHERO'S NAME

CREATE a TOTALLY WEIRD SUPER VILLAIN!

DESIGN and COLOR their costume!

What are their powers?

_____
_____
_____

How did they become evil?

What's their weakness?

_____
_____
_____

_____
_____
_____

Where are they from?

_____
_____
_____

Are they human, alien, or robot?

Where is their hideout?

_____

* Turn the page over to write more information about this villain!

_____

It's the ... MYSTERIOUS OLD PHOTO!

Little Scotty Etler's family moved into a house in Taboo, Texas. He went to the attic and found this old photo taken in 1895. At first glance he saw a smiling family. But then he noticed something in the background.... Something totally weird that shouldn't be there. What is it? Draw it and color the photo in OLD-TIME colors like GRAY or TAN!

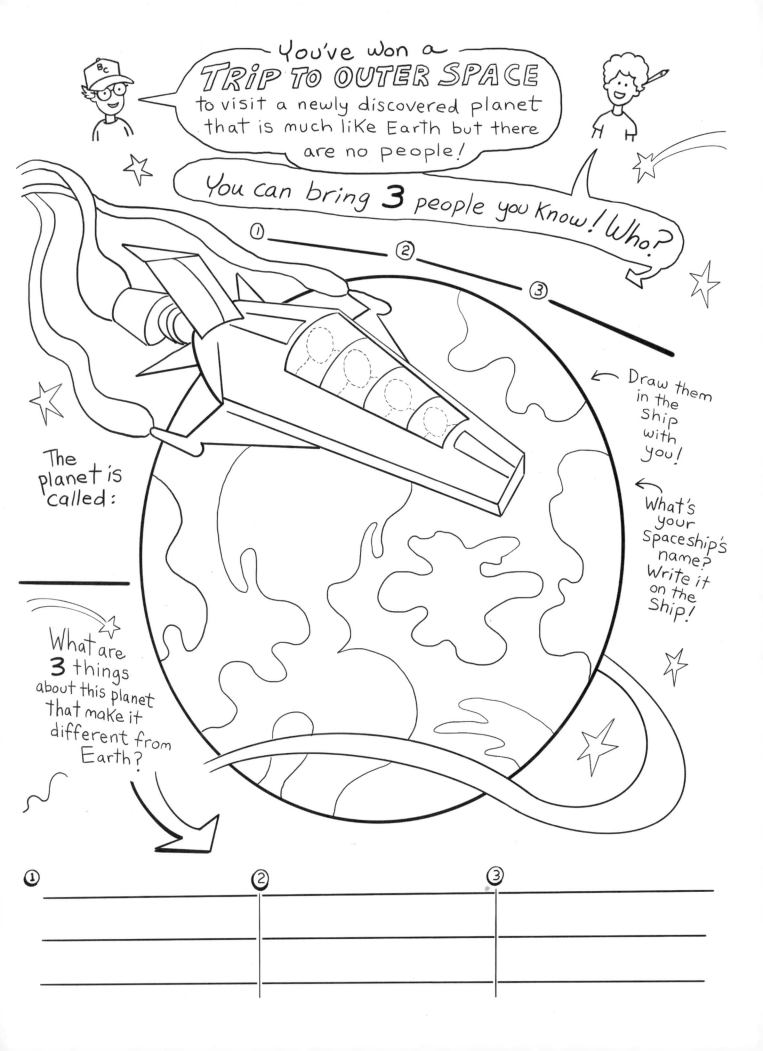

The Adventures of Mr. SNIFFLES!

Color this **TOTALLY WEIRD** comic and fill in the blank word balloons!

WRITE A STORY!

The field trip on the Magellan was a blast until the giant octopus attacked ...or so it seemed! Mrs. Meserve's class appeared doomed until they noticed the octopus was smiling. That's when something totally weird happened. What was it?

Write it down here!

Your town has been overtaken by one of the following . . . . .

Jellyfish   Giant Spiders   Zany birds   Wild dogs

PiCK ONE and WRiTE a TOTALLY WEIRD STORY ABOUT a HERO who saves the town!

"It was a hot, dry day in the town of _____ when all of a sudden...

* If you need more space, turn the page and finish!

ABOUT THE AUTHORS

T.M. Murphy is the author of the Belltown Mystery Series and *Saving Santa's Seals*. Murphy has been featured in *101 Highly Successful Novelists*, and chosen by *Cape Cod Life Magazine* as One of the 400 Cape Cod People Who Brighten Our Lives. He spends his winters touring schools and his summers teaching young writers at The Writers' Shack in his hometown of Falmouth, Massachusetts. Visit www.facebook.com/TheJustWriteItClass.

Mark Penta is a freelance illustrator and Hartford Art School graduate. His work has been published by Dell Magazines, Andrews McMeel, and featured on the Belltown Mystery book covers. He is the author/illustrator of several picture books, including *Cape Cod Invasion!* which was named a "Must-have product" by *Cape Cod Life Magazine*. He has taught drawing lessons to all ages, both privately and at schools like R.I.S.D. He also runs a fun and successful drawing service at private parties and corporate events. Visit www.MarkPenta.com.

Learn more about their Totally Weird Activity Books at
www.TotallyWeirdActivityBooks.com and
www.facebook.com/TotallyWeirdActivityBooks.